T0026060

HOW TO SEE

THICH NHAT HANH

**PARALLAX
PRESS**

BERKELEY, CALIFORNIA

Parallax Press
P.O. Box 7355
Berkeley, California 94707
parallax.org

Parallax Press is the publishing division of
the Plum Village Community of Engaged Buddhism, Inc.
© 2019 Plum Village Community of Engaged
Buddhism, Inc.
Printed in the United States of America

Cover and text design by Debbie Berne
Illustrations by Jason DeAntonis

The material in this book comes from previously
published books and unpublished Dharma talks by
Thich Nhat Hanh.

ISBN: 978-1-946764-33-1

Library of Congress Cataloging-in-Publication Data
Names: Nhat Hanh, Thich, author.
Title: How to see / Thich Nhat Hanh.
Description: Berkeley, California : Parallax Press, 2019. |
    Includes bibliographical references and index.
Identifiers: LCCN 2019017539 (print) | LCCN 2019021366
    (ebook) | ISBN 9781946764348 (ebook) | ISBN
    9781946764331 (alk. paper)
Subjects: LCSH: Buddhism—Philosophy. | Buddhist
    philosophy. | Mindfulness (Psychology)—Miscellanea.
Classification: LCC BQ9800.T5392 (ebook) | LCC
    BQ9800.T5392 N454455 2019 (print) | DDC
    294.3/4435—dc23
LC record available at https://lccn.loc.gov/2019017539

2 3 4 5 / 23 22 21 20 19

CONTENTS

Notes on Seeing 7

Practices for Looking Deeply 113

NOTES
ON SEEING

If you are a poet, you will see clearly that
there is a cloud floating in this sheet of paper.
Without the cloud there can be no rain;
without water, the trees cannot grow; and
without trees, you cannot make paper. So the
cloud is in here. The existence of this page
is dependent upon the existence of a cloud.
Paper and cloud are so close.

WATER REFLECTING

The clear still water of a mountain lake reflects the mountain and the sky with pristine clarity. You can do the same. If you are calm and still enough, you can reflect the mountain, the blue sky, and the moon exactly as they are. You reflect whatever you see just as it is, without distorting anything.

RIVER OF PERCEPTIONS

In each of us there is a river of perceptions.
Perceptions arise, stay for a period of time, and
cease to be. When our mind is not calm, we
do not see clearly. Like the surface of a lake
on a windy day, the image we see is distorted.
Our perceptions are often erroneous, and
cause us to suffer and cause others to suffer.
It is very helpful to look deeply into the nature
of our perceptions, without being too sure of
anything. When we are too sure, we suffer.
When we ask ourselves, "Are you sure?" we
have a chance to look again and see if our
perception is correct or not.

SIGN OR REALITY?

We are convinced that our perceptions are correct and complete, yet often they are not. In the Chinese character for perception, the upper part is "sign" or "appearance," and the lower part is "mind." When we perceive something, an image of that thing—a sign—is created in our mind, and in many cases that sign is illusory. It is very easy to confuse our mental image of something with its reality. It is important not to be too sure of our perceptions.

THE SNAKE

Imagine you are walking in the twilight and you see a snake. You scream and run into the house to get your friends, and all of you rush outside with a flashlight. But when you shine your light on the snake, you discover it isn't a snake at all, it's just a piece of rope. Mistaking the rope for a snake is a wrong perception. Mindfulness helps us avoid being caught by our wrong perceptions.

SEEING THE TRUE NATURE OF THINGS

The practice of full awareness is to look deeply in order to see the true nature of things and go beyond our inaccurate perceptions. Seeing a rope as a snake, we may cry out in fear. Fear is a feeling brought about as a result of our wrong perception. Our perceptions are often inaccurate and can bring about strong feelings and reactions and cause much unnecessary suffering. Once we have seen the true nature of the object of our fear, our fear will vanish.

THE SOURCE OF OUR PERCEPTIONS

The source of perception, our way of seeing, lies in our unconscious mind. Most of our perceptions are erroneous. They carry with them all the errors of subjectivity. We praise or blame, are happy or complain depending on our perceptions. Our perceptions are made of many things, including our afflictions, such as craving, anger, and ignorance, as well as our habit energies and past experiences. Whether we are happy or whether we suffer depends largely on our perceptions. It is important to look deeply into our perceptions and recognize their source.

GOOD OR BAD LUCK?

One day a farmer went to the field and found that his horse had run away. The people in the village said, "Oh, what bad luck!" The next day the horse returned with two other horses and the village people said, "What good fortune!" Then the farmer's son was thrown from one of the horses and broke his leg. The villagers expressed their sympathy, "How unfortunate." Soon after, a war broke out and young men from the village were being drafted. But because the farmer's son had a broken leg, he was the only one not drafted. Now the village people told the farmer that his son's broken leg was really "good luck."

It is not possible to judge any event as simply fortunate or unfortunate, good or bad, as this age-old story shows. You must travel throughout all of time and space to know the true impact of any event. Every success contains some difficulties, and every failure contributes to increased wisdom or future success. Every event is both fortunate and unfortunate. Fortunate and unfortunate, good and bad, these concepts exist only in our mind.

THE CLOUD IN YOUR TEA

Imagine a cloud transforming herself into rain.
The rain will nourish many trees and plants.
We should be able to recognize the cloud
in its new forms as trees and plants of many
kinds. Looking deeply into the rain, ice, or
snow, we can recognize the cloud. Looking
deeply into your tea, you can recognize the
cloud. When you drink your tea mindfully,
you know you are drinking a cloud—how
wonderful! When children eat an ice cream,
they are also eating a cloud. This is the way
we train ourselves to look at reality, with the
eye of formlessness, signlessness; it means
transcending the appearance, the sign, to
touch the ultimate reality. If you don't have the

eyes of signlessness you cannot recognize the cloud in your tea, in your ice cream, in the rain, or in the vegetables. We can all train ourselves to look with the eyes of signlessness.

LOOKING INTO THE ROSE

Suppose we look deeply at a rose. With some concentration and mindfulness, we can see that the rose is made of only non-rose elements. What do we see in the rose? We see a cloud, because we know that without the cloud, there would be no rain, and without the rain, the rose couldn't grow. So a cloud is a non-rose element that we can recognize if we look deeply into the rose. Next, we can see sunshine, which is also crucial for the rose to grow. The sunshine is another non-rose element present in the rose. If you took the sunshine and the cloud out of the rose, there would be no rose left. If we continue like this, we see many other non-rose elements within the rose, including the minerals, the soil, the farmer, the gardener, and so on. The whole cosmos has come together to produce the wonder we call a rose. A rose cannot be by herself alone. A rose has to inter-be with the whole cosmos. This is the insight we call interbeing. When looking at a rose, if we can see all the non-rose elements that make up the rose, then we can truly touch the reality of the rose. No matter what we look at, if we can see that it is made up of everything in the universe that is not itself, then we touch the true reality of that thing, its nonself nature. There is a Zen proverb. Before I began to look deeply, mountains were mountains and rivers were rivers. Once I began to look deeply, mountains were no longer mountains and rivers were no longer rivers. Now, as I have practiced looking deeply for some time, mountains are again mountains and rivers are again rivers. When we see the signless nature of phenomena, we see things as they are.

TRANSCENDING SIGNS

Everything is born from our mind, from our way of looking. Deception is born from signs, external appearances. According to the Diamond Sutra, "In a place where something can be distinguished by signs, in that place there is deception." In other words, where there is perception, there is deception. Our practice is to transcend signs to see more clearly. Until we look deeply into reality and discover its true nature of impermanence and interconnectedness, we will continue to be fooled by signs. When we transcend signs, notions, and ideas, we are in touch with the ultimate reality. We need to see through the outer form to be in touch with the substance. When we're no longer deceived by signs, our perceptions become insight.

THE THING IN ITSELF

When we think of a table, we see an image of that table in our mind. But we must remember that our concept is not the thing itself. It's just our perception, which might in fact be very different from the table. A termite may perceive a table as a feast, and a physicist may perceive it as a mass of rapidly moving particles. The more we practice looking deeply, the more accurate our perceptions can be. But they are still perceptions.

EVERYTHING IS POSSIBLE

Nagarjuna, the second century Buddhist
teacher, said, "Thanks to emptiness, everything
is possible." Emptiness is another term for
nonself; when we say things are empty,
it means they are without a separate self.
Nonself and impermanence are two sides of
reality; impermanence is looking at reality in
terms of time, and nonself is looking at reality in
terms of space. When we look deeply into our
fears, we can see our desire for permanence
and our fear of change. But impermanence
and nonself are not something negative.
Impermanence means transformation at every
moment. Therefore we can say, "Thanks to
impermanence, everything is possible."

THE BOAT

A man was rowing his boat upstream when suddenly he saw another boat coming down stream toward him. He shouted, "Watch out!" but the boat ran right into him, nearly sinking his boat. The man became angry and began to shout, but when he looked closely, he saw that there was no one in the other boat. The boat had drifted downstream by itself. When our perceptions are incorrect, they can cause us a lot of unnecessary suffering. We look at things deeply in order to understand their true nature, so that we will not be misled or suffer unnecessarily.

IT'S ALL IN THE MIND

All phenomena are objects of mind, they're not objective realities. When we perceive something, that thing is the object of our consciousness. There needs to be both a perceiver and an object of mind for a perception to be obtained. The world is just an object of mind. When you see a mountain, that mountain is the object of your mind, the object of your perception; it's not something separate from your consciousness. Usually we think that there's a subjective consciousness inside us that's reaching out to the world of reality outside. But this is a wrong view. We have to see that both subject and object of perception rely on each other and manifest at the same time. The object can never be separated from the mind that observes or meditates upon it.

INTERCONNECTION

One day, when I was doing Qi Gong exercises in front of a tree, it occurred to me that the tree had a lot to offer me, and I had a lot to offer the tree. The tree offers me beauty, shade, and oxygen. I offer the tree my breath, my appreciation, and my joy. The tree and I are interconnected. When we look at a human being, we can look in exactly the same way, without exaggerating what is there or imagining what is not there. Sometimes we expect too much, we want to idealize what we see. If we can acknowledge reality as it is without exaggerating or imagining, we will suffer less.

CONFUSING SIGNS WITH REALITY

It is very easy to confuse our mental image of something with its reality. The process of mistaking our perceptions for reality is so subtle that it is very difficult to know that it is going on. Practicing mindfulness is the way we can avoid this confusion.

I AM FROM THE CENTER

At a peace rally in Philadelphia in 1966, a reporter asked me, "Are you from North or South Vietnam?" If I had said I was from the North, he would have seen me as pro-communist, and if I had said I was from the South, he would have seen me as pro-American. So I told him, "I am from the Center." I wanted to help him let go of his notions, his perceptions, and encounter the reality that was right in front of him. This is the language of Zen.

TOUCHING PEACE

The practice of mindfulness of breathing,
of sitting and walking in mindfulness, trains
us to generate an energy that can help us
be stable and calm. When we touch peace
within ourselves, everything becomes real.
We become fully ourselves, fully alive in the
present moment, and the tree, the flower, our
child, our loved ones, and everything else
reveal themselves to us in their full splendor.

BEYOND VIEWS

Relatively speaking, there are right views
and wrong views. But if we look more deeply,
we see that all views are wrong views. Any
view is just from one point; that's why it's
called a point of view. If we go to another
point, we have a different perspective, we
see things differently, and we realize that our
first view was not entirely accurate. We need
to continue expanding the boundaries of
our understanding or we will be imprisoned
by our views. For example, if we are able to
remove the notion of permanence, we may
still get caught in the notion of impermanence;
we have to be free from both notions.
This is why we say that Right View means
removing all kinds of views, even the views of
impermanence, nonself, and interbeing.

MINDFULNESS AND CONCENTRATION

Mindfulness is the capacity of being aware. It is a nonjudgmental awareness of all that is happening inside us and around us. It helps us be fully present in the here and now, which is the foundation of happiness. With mindfulness we can enjoy the present moment, the only moment of life available to us. Mindfulness increases concentration, which allows us to see things more deeply and clearly, and we stop being victims of wrong perceptions. We create less suffering for ourselves and for other people. We begin to taste the joy of living and know how to help others to enjoy their daily lives, too. We cannot force people to practice mindfulness, but if we practice mindfulness ourselves and become happier people, we can inspire others to practice.

STOPPING AND LOOKING DEEPLY

The way to look deeply is to stop whatever we're doing and truly concentrate on what we're observing. Meditation is not to avoid problems or run away from difficulties. We practice to have enough strength to confront problems effectively. To do this, we must be calm, fresh, and solid. This is why we need to practice the art of stopping. When we learn to stop, we become calmer and our mind becomes clearer. Sitting and following our breathing, even for a few minutes, is already good. Stopping brings body and mind together, back to the here and now. Stop what you are doing and quiet your restless mind. You will naturally become more solid and concentrated, and you will see everything more clearly.

APPLE JUICE MEDITATION

One day four children were playing outside at
my Sweet Potato hermitage in France. Thanh
Thuy, a four-year-old girl I was looking after,
was among them. The children were thirsty
so I offered them each a glass of homemade
apple juice which contained some pulp. Thanh
Thuy did not like the look of the cloudy juice
and refused to drink it. She ran off to play but
came back after a while and asked for water.
I showed her the apple juice and urged her to
drink it. She saw the pulp had settled, and the
juice now looked clear and delicious. "Is this
the same glass or a different one?" she asked.
"Was it meditating like you?" I laughed, "Let's
say I am imitating the apple juice when I sit;
that is closer to the truth." If you know how to
sit stably and follow your in- and out-breath,

then after some time you become peaceful and clear, like the apple juice. When we focus our mind on our breathing, our mind can settle. Our habitual thinking and worrying subside, and we can see people and situations more clearly. When we are still, it gives insight a chance to arise.

WAKING FROM THE DREAM

It's easy to see that a dream isn't real. But
when we're awake, it's not so easy to see
what's real. What we believe to be external
reality may only be a construction of our
mind. We think we're awake but in fact we
continue to dream. Most of the time we are
sleepwalking. For example, although we know
intellectually that things are impermanent
and subject to change, we live as though our
body is permanent; we think we will never die.
Even if we understand that a separate "self"
is a misperception, most of our thinking is
based on seeing things as having a separate,
individual self. This lends us a certain sense
of security, but in fact it is based on wrong
perception. Many philosophers, scientists,

and spiritual teachers search for an absolute truth because they don't trust their own perceptions. They have the impression that although they are awake they are living in a dream. We all have the ability to wake up from that dream, because we all have the seed of mindfulness.

TAKING OUR TIME

To meditate is not to run away from life but to take the time to look deeply into ourselves or into a situation to see what is truly going on. Meditation is an opportunity to take care of our body and our mind; this is very important. We allow ourselves the time to calm our thinking, to sit, to walk, to breathe—not doing anything, just going back to ourselves and to what is around us. We allow ourselves time to release the tension in our body and our mind. Then, when we are peaceful and calm, we can take time to look deeply into ourselves and into the situation we are in. When our mind and body are calm we can see the situation more clearly. Our view is not obscured or distorted.

TOUCHING IMPERMANENCE

We have all had the experience at some time
of reading something and fooling ourselves
into believing we have understood what we
have read. But upon rereading or referring
back to it, we see that we haven't really
absorbed or understood it at all. The same
is true of looking deeply. We may think it's
easy to see that a flower is impermanent,
that its beauty will soon fade, and its petals
wither and die. Intellectually, we accept the
flower's impermanence. But it's not by using
our intellect that we truly touch impermanence.
We have to touch the nature of impermanence
deeply in order to go beyond our notion of
impermanence. Mindfulness and concentration
are the powers that allow us to go deeply into
the true nature of things and bring forth insight.

OBSERVING TRANSFORMATION

A child may believe she is a totally different
person from her mother, but in fact she is the
continuation of her mother, she is her mother.
We can train ourselves to recognize reality
beyond the forms we're used to perceiving.
Looking at a young cornstalk, at first you cannot
see the seed of corn that gave life to the plant.
But looking closer, you can see the seed in
her new form: the cornstalk. Transcending the
notions of sameness and otherness we see the
truth. Observing in this way is a deep practice.

LETTING GO

Most of our feelings and emotions arise
from narrow perceptions and incomplete
understanding. Our ways of looking, listening,
reacting, and judging make us and our loved
ones suffer. We have ideas about happiness
and suffering that we can't let go of, though
we know that by letting go of them we'll
be happier and more peaceful in body and
mind, and the painful feelings and emotions
would no longer have a basis to arise. We
tend to think that if we let go, we'll lose the
things that make us happy. But the opposite
is true. The more we let go, the happier we
become. Letting go doesn't mean we let go
of everything. We don't let go of reality. But
we let go of our wrong ideas and perceptions
about reality.

RIGHT VIEW

Our "view" is our way of understanding the world; it is based on our perceptions. Right View is a view that transcends dualistic thinking, a living insight into the reality of life. Right View is the first element of the Noble Eightfold Path and the foundation of all right thinking, speech, and actions. If we don't have Right View, our thoughts, speech, and actions will not be skillful and will lead to more suffering. The eight elements of the Path nourish and depend on each other. For example, Right Thinking and Right Speech are based on Right View and at the same time they nourish Right View. Our happiness, and the happiness of those around us, depends on our degree of Right View. With our daily practice of mindfulness we nourish the seed of Right View.

IDENTIFYING SEEDS

All our potential states of mind exist as seeds
in our unconscious mind (store consciousness).
Practicing mindfulness helps us identify all
the seeds and water those that are most
wholesome. When one person approaches
us, we may feel aversion. But when another
walks by, we may feel drawn to her right away.
Something in each of them touches a seed in
us. If we love our mother deeply but feel tense
when we think of our father, that naturally
affects how we respond to others. In this way,
we can recognize the seeds that are in us—
seeds of love for our mother and seeds of hurt
vis-à-vis our father. When we become aware of
the seeds in our store consciousness, we will
not be surprised by our own behavior or the
behavior of others.

ALL THE SEEDS ARE WITHIN US

We all have the ability to distinguish the
wholesome from the unwholesome seeds that
exist in the depths of our consciousness. We
all have all the possible seeds within us; they
contain all the different feelings, thoughts, and
perceptions we may have. If you are loyal, it is
because you have the seed of loyalty in you.
But don't think that the seed of betrayal isn't
in you as well. If you live in an environment
where your seed of loyalty is sufficiently
watered, you will become a loyal person. But
if your seed of betrayal is watered, you may
betray even those you love.

WATERING WHOLESOME SEEDS

Sometimes we see our children doing things that we know will cause them to suffer in the future, but when we try to tell them, they won't listen. All we can do is to water the seeds of Right View in them, and then later, in a difficult moment, they may benefit from our guidance. We cannot explain a mango to someone who has never tasted one. No matter how well we describe it, we cannot give someone else the direct experience. They have to taste it for themselves. As soon as we say a single word, they are already caught. Right View cannot be described. We can only point in the correct direction. Right View cannot even be transmitted by a teacher. A teacher can help us identify the seed of Right View that is already in our garden, and help us have the confidence to practice, to entrust that seed to the soil of our daily life. But we are the gardener. We have to learn how to water the wholesome seeds that are in us so they will bloom into the flowers of Right View. The instrument for watering wholesome seeds is mindful living—mindful breathing, mindful walking, living each moment of our day in mindfulness.

THE SEED OF INSIGHT

The seed of insight is in us, but it's obscured
by layers of ignorance, sorrow, and disappoint-
ment. When we practice mindfulness, we see
the seed of awakening in everyone, including
ourselves. In the process of learning, reflecting,
and looking deeply, our view becomes increas-
ingly wise. When we practice mindful living,
Right View will blossom. With Right View, we
see the way to go, and our seeing gives us
faith and energy, based on our real experience.
If we feel better after walking meditation,
we'll have the determination to continue the
practice. When we see walking meditation
bringing peace to others, we'll have more faith
in the practice. With patience, we can discover
the joy of life that is around us.

BELIEF IN OUR PERCEPTIONS

A young widower returned home one day
to find his house burned down and his five-
year-old son missing. Nearby was the charred
corpse of a child he believed to be his son;
he wept bitterly. After the child's cremation,
he kept the ashes in a bag around his neck
and carried them with him day and night.
But his son hadn't perished; he'd been taken
off by bandits. One day he escaped and
returned to his father's new house. Arriving
late at night, he knocked at the door. Who's
there?" asked the father. "It's me, your son."
"That's impossible. My son is dead." The father
persisted in his belief and would not open the
door. In the end the boy had to leave, and the
father lost his son forever.

When we believe something to be the absolute truth, we cannot be open to new ideas. Even if the truth comes knocking at our door, we will not let it in. We need to remain open so that truth has a chance to enter. Our wrong perceptions can be very costly. They bring about suspicion, fear, anger, hatred, and despair, which can give rise to actions based on that wrong perception. When the wrong perception is removed, suspicion, fear, anger, hatred, and despair are also removed, and happiness is possible again. When conflicts arise between two people, we need to stop and question our perceptions. With the practice of good communication, deep listening, and loving speech, we can help each other remove wrong perceptions. This is also true for conflicts between groups of people and nations.

SEEDS OF SUFFERING

When we look deeply at a flower, we can
see the non-flower elements that help it to
manifest—the clouds, the earth, the gardener,
and the soil. When we look deeply at our pain,
we see that our suffering is not ours alone.
It is also made of many non-self elements.
Many seeds of suffering have been handed
down to us by our ancestors, our parents, and
our society. Being aware of the seeds of our
suffering is the first step in their transformation.

ARE YOU SURE?

We are quite sure that our perception of reality is correct. We may think someone hates us or wants to hurt us but this may be nothing more than a creation of our mind. Believing that our perception is reality, we act on that belief; this can be very dangerous. A wrong perception can create countless problems. All our suffering arises from our failure to recognize things as they are. We should be humble and ask, "Am I sure?" and then allow space and time for our perceptions to grow deeper and clearer. In medical practice these days, physicians and caregivers remind each other not to be too sure of anything. Even if you think you are certain, "Check it again," they urge each other. We, too, can do the same.

SEEING OUR STRENGTHS AND WEAKNESSES

Looking deeply into yourself you may notice some strengths that you have inherited from your parents and ancestors. You are their continuation; they've passed these things on to you. They're not yours alone. We don't need to be too proud. Your fear, anger, and discrimination have also been transmitted to you by parents, ancestors, and society. We don't need to judge. Your parents and ancestors weren't able to transform all their shortcomings, so they have passed their difficulties on to you. Now you have a chance to transform so that you will not transmit them to your children. This way of looking at yourself and others will give rise to understanding, compassion, and a desire to transform.

LET OTHERS BE YOUR MIRROR

Our family members and friends are like mirrors. Practicing with humility and openness, we can make great progress by making use of the mirrors that are held up to us. In confronting our weaknesses and finding ways to overcome them, we will feel light. When we observe a particular behavior in ourselves, we can ask others for support: "Dear friend, dear brother, dear sister, please help me. When you see that my behavior is not kind or skillful, please let me know." When we ask for support like this, our family members and friends will have great respect and love for us and they will be encouraged to do the same.

UNDERSTANDING ILL-BEING

We shouldn't try to run away from our suffering. Embrace your suffering and look deeply into it. With deep looking, understanding will arise, and compassion will be born. If we have already understood our own pain, it will be much easier to understand the pain of another person. If we understand the nature of the ill-being inside us, it will be much easier to understand the nature of the ill being around us. In a civilization where we are so focused on technology and material wealth, there is little room for compassion. Yet understanding and compassion are what make happiness possible.

OUR OWN CONTRIBUTION

Looking deeply into our suffering, we can ask ourselves how we have contributed to it. This doesn't mean our suffering isn't real, just that we have the capacity to lessen it instead of adding to it, and that we can even transform it. When we have a conflict with someone else, we also need to look deeply to see how we have contributed to the difficulty that has arisen. We have our part to play. We can ask ourselves, "In what ways have I contributed to this situation?" This is the kind of deep looking that can bring healing and reconciliation.

NO BLAMING

When we grow a lemon tree, we want it to
be vigorous and beautiful. But if it doesn't
thrive, we don't blame the tree. We observe
it in order to understand why it isn't growing
well. Perhaps we have not taken care of it well
enough. We know it would be odd to blame a
lemon tree and yet we blame human beings
when they are not growing well. But human
beings are not very different from lemon trees.
If we take good care of them, they will grow
well. Blaming never helps.

MAKING PEACE

When we're angry with someone, it's because we feel hurt. We're unable to see the many elements that make up that person. We don't realize they may be acting out of habit energy transmitted to them from their ancestors. Once we see this, we can accept the person more easily. This is true concerning ourselves as well. When we can see within us all the elements that have been handed down to us from our parents, ancestors, and our environment, we can let go of much of our self-judgment and criticism, and also stop judging and criticizing others. We see, "Ah, that is my father in me who is judging my friend." Our ancestors continue in us each day. With this understanding, we can find a way to undo the difficulties we have with others and make peace.

UNILATERAL RECONCILIATION

We're often caught in images of our past
suffering, so we easily develop wrong
perceptions and react in ways that bring more
suffering. We may be angry with someone
because we believe they want to make us
suffer. This perception brings about anger
and we may act in a way that will lead to
more suffering for all involved. Instead, we
can use mindful breathing and walking to
calm ourselves and generate awareness and
insight. Breathing in and out, we recognize
there is suffering and wrong perceptions
within us and in the other person. With this
insight, healing begins. Reconciliation can be
unilateral. Your understanding will affect the
other person even if they don't yet know how
to recognize and handle their suffering.

THE INTERVENTION OF INSIGHT

Anger is an organic, living thing, and so is love. If we know how to handle our anger it can turn into love, just as when we know how to take care of our compost, we can transform it into a beautiful rose. Is garbage negative or positive? It can be positive, if we know how to handle it. Anger is the same. We do not need to get rid of it. When we're able to see someone's suffering and understand their situation, we have another way of looking at them, and compassion arises. Compassion transforms our anger and we no longer want to punish the other person. Thanks to our insight, we can correct our wrong perceptions. Instead of anger, fear, and despair, we have compassion and the willingness to help the other person.

FORGIVENESS

When you can see all the causes that led to
another person's actions, forgiveness arises
naturally. You can't force yourself to forgive.
Only when you truly understand the causes
and conditions that have made someone act
the way they did, can you have compassion
and forgive them. Then, forgiveness and
release arise naturally. Forgiveness is the
fruit of awareness and insight, the result of
really seeing someone and understanding
their suffering. Understanding someone else's
challenges and suffering, you can accept and
even love that person just as they are.

THIS IS BECAUSE THAT IS

Understanding the essential nature of inter-being is to see that this is like this because that is like that. Everything comes to be because of causes and conditions. This arises because that arises. For there to be a mother, there has to be a child; and if there is a child, there has to be a mother. We only exist in this interconnected way. With this insight, we see clearly and we can be more effective. This is because that is; this is not because that is not. This is the insight of interbeing. Nothing can exist on its own. Everything in the world is interdependent.

DOUBT

Doubt can be helpful. If you don't doubt, you have no chance to discover the true nature of what is. According to Zen Buddhism, the greater your doubt, the greater will be your enlightenment. So doubt can be a good thing. If you are too sure, if you always have conviction, then you may be caught in your wrong perception for a long time.

OUR IDEA OF HAPPINESS

We have an idea of happiness. We may believe that only certain conditions will make us happy. But it is often our very idea of happiness that prevents us from being happy. The conditions for happiness are already there, available inside and around us. We have eyes that can see, legs that can walk, lungs that can breathe. All the wonders of life are available in the present moment—the sunshine, the fresh air, the trees, the multitude of colors and forms all around us. The essential thing is to be aware. If we open our eyes, we will see.

SEEING OUR BELOVED ONE

We are all victims of wrong perception. When we are in love with someone we are full of wrong perceptions about that person. We are in love with the image of our beloved rather than the actual person. Once we begin to discover the reality of the other person, which doesn't quite correspond with the image we have of them, we're often disappointed. We need to come home to ourselves, to look deeply and compassionately in order to understand ourselves and accept our short-comings. Only when we can embrace ourself with understanding and compassion, can we accept and be patient and compassionate with the one we love. This is when the practice of true love begins, when we learn to understand and accept the other person as they are.

KEEPING LOVE ALIVE

Looking deeply at each other we can see each other's deepest concerns and aspirations, and we can also see each other's fears, suffering, and loneliness. When we see and understand the pain and suffering in ourselves and in the other, understanding and compassion begin to grow. These two energies have the power to heal and transform us. This is the secret to nourishing our love. We see that in the world nothing can survive without food. The same is true with love. However beautiful our love is, it is impermanent, so we need to learn how to feed our love with the energy of understanding and compassion. Only when we know how to look deeply at each other, and how to look deeply at ourselves, can we generate these two precious energies.

MIND AND BODY ARE ONE

Whatever happens to the body also happens to the mind. When we look at the body as an item of consumption, an object of desire, we haven't truly seen the body. Our own body, and the body of another, should be treated with utmost respect. The body is as sacred as the mind. When we touch someone else's body, we touch their mind and their soul.

THE NATURE OF CRAVING AND HAPPINESS

Much of our suffering depends on our perceptions and desire. Whenever we don't get what we want, we suffer. But the truth is that sometimes we do get what we want and yet we suffer even more. Maybe it's not what we thought it was, it doesn't have the desired effect, or it changes something else in our lives for the worse. Sometimes, after we get the thing we thought we wanted, we don't treasure it anymore, and we want something else instead.

People tend to think of happiness in terms of having plenty of fame, power, wealth, and sensual pleasures. But we know that craving these objects can bring a lot of suffering. So we need to have a very different understanding of happiness. If we cultivate peace in ourselves, then clarity, compassion, and courage will arise. We have to look deeply in order to see the true nature of the object of our craving. When we recognize it clearly, it will lose its appeal, and we will be free.

MINDFULNESS PROTECTS US

When we drive through the city, we are constantly consuming things, whether we want to or not. Advertising penetrates our consciousness and the consciousness of our children, who are even less able than we are to filter these sources of toxic consumption. In modern life, we are exposed to many violent or exciting images, sounds, films, TV programs, and articles that either give rise to fear and despair or incite craving. Without mindfulness, we don't have a skin to shield us, and what we see and hear assaults us and penetrates our consciousness. With mindfulness, we have a means to protect ourselves and to be aware of what we are consuming through our senses.

INDIVIDUAL AND COLLECTIVE CONSCIOUSNESS

We are influenced by ways of thinking and we consume the views of other people in many ways. Individual consciousness is made of collective consciousness, and collective consciousness is made of individual consciousness. It is our consciousness that designs our world.

SEEING BEYOND LABELS

Sometimes people have a certain idea or way of looking at things, and they want to put you in a box. But what happens if you don't belong in any of their categories? It's the reality of the thing that matters, and not the word we use to describe it. A name is merely a conventional designation, it's not the reality in itself. We must train ourselves to look at each other beyond labels to see each other's true nature.

ACCESS TO REALITY

Within store consciousness, we have direct access to reality, to suchness, to things as they are. In every one of us lies the basic wisdom that can directly touch reality itself. Nevertheless, we often feel attachment or aversion based on prior experience. We classify what we perceive according to the boxes we already have in our store consciousness. We compare the present with what we have experienced in the past and we seem to recognize it. We paint the new information with the old colors we already have inside us. This is why most of the time we don't have direct access to reality, to things as they are.

IN TOUCH WITH THINGS AS THEY ARE

We know that having a crush on someone
is not the same as really loving that person.
First we create an image, and then we fall in
love with that image. The object of our love
is not the thing in itself. It's merely a mental
construct, a representation of reality, but
not reality itself. This is true whether we are
looking at a mountain, at a star, or at other
people. Usually, we are just dealing with
representations and living in the realm of
illusion. But we have the capacity to touch
reality itself. This takes some training, because
many of us have lost this capacity. The good
news is that, with the practice of mindfulness,
we can restore our capacity for touching
suchness and seeing our loved ones as they
truly are.

THE FIVE UNIVERSAL MENTAL FORMATIONS

Contact between a subject and object of perception—between the observer and the thing being observed—always waters a seed in store consciousness and brings about a reaction. Contact is the first of the five mental formations, or states of mind, called "universal," because they are always functioning, always present in our consciousness. The other four are attention, feeling, perception, and volition. Together they form a neural pathway. For example, when our eyes come into *contact* with something that looks like a snake, our *attention* is drawn to it, and we may *feel* afraid. *Perceiving* it to be a snake, we may have the *volition* to run away. All this happens so quickly we are not aware of it.

HABIT ENERGY

In our brain are many neural pathways along which we frequently travel, habitual responses we have to an object of perception. With the practice of mindfulness, concentration, and insight, we can intervene in the sequence of steps between contact and volition, and open up a new neural pathway that replaces our habitual, automatic response, a new pathway that takes us down a different route, leading to more understanding and well-being.

CREATING A NEW
NEURAL PATHWAY

Suppose you are reaching for something
sweet to eat. But because you've learned
mindfulness, you suddenly become aware of
what you are doing, and you ask, "Why am I
reaching for a cookie? I'm not hungry." We take
the time to breathe. One in-breath can make
all the difference. You may discover that there
is some worry, loneliness, or irritation in you,
so you're automatically reaching for something
to eat to cover up the unpleasant feeling. This
has become a habit and has created a neural
pathway in your brain that often leads to
suffering. Bringing mindfulness, concentration,
and insight into the process of perception, you
can create a new neural pathway that leads to
understanding and more happiness.

CHECKING PERCEPTIONS

When someone says or does something that
gives you a painful feeling, you may have the
perception that this person is trying to make
you suffer. But maybe the truth isn't like that.
Maybe that person was simply not mindful or
they didn't sleep well the night before. Their
words or actions may give you the impression
that they are being unkind to you, that they
are indeed unkind, and this perception may
make you want to say something unkind back.
If we think the other person is cruel, we often
want to say something even more cruel to
punish them because we think we will suffer
less that way. This isn't wise but it's how most
of us respond. So we need to check our
perceptions. We can ask the other person
for help.

NO DISCRIMINATION

My right hand has the wisdom of nondiscrimination. It has a name, "right hand," and it has
five fingers. My left hand has a name, "left
hand," and it also has five fingers. My right
hand can practice calligraphy, invite the bell,
and it has written all my poems, except one,
when I didn't have a pen so I borrowed a type-
writer, put an old envelope in it, and typed with
both hands. My right hand has no complex of
superiority. It never says, "Dear left hand, I see
you're not very useful. All those poems—it's
me who has written them." It doesn't discriminate. It's at peace with my left hand. They
never fight. My left hand has no inferiority
complex and no equality complex either. She
doesn't compare; she doesn't suffer at all.

THE PRICE OF A WRONG PERCEPTION

I know a young man who suffered terribly because of a wrong perception. His father, upon returning home from a trip, learned that his wife was pregnant. He suspected the child had been fathered by a neighbor who had been very helpful to his wife while he had been away. He became icy and distant from his wife. She had no idea why, and she suffered a lot. The child grew up in that atmosphere of suspicion and wrong perception. When he was twelve, his uncle visited and commented that the boy looked just like his father. Only then did the father accept him as his son. But much damage had been done in all those years to the whole family, and the extent of the damage continues to reveal itself.

A wrong perception can be very costly. We have to learn to see things more clearly in our daily life and avoid wrong perceptions as much as possible. We must always go to the other person and ask if our perception is correct. The father was caught in his pride and didn't have the courage to go to his wife. Pride has no place in true love. If you suspect something, go to the other person and say, "I suffer. Please help. Please tell me why you did (or said) that." Don't be like this father and cause suffering to yourself, to the ones you love, and to many others. Ask, "Are you sure?" Are you sure of your perceptions? Be willing to release your present view. You will avoid much suffering if you're open to reexamining and exploring your views.

UNITY AND DIVERSITY

All phenomena are interdependent. Yet when
we think of a speck of dust, a flower, or a
human being, our mind sees these things as
individual phenomena. If we truly realize the
interdependent nature of the dust, the flower,
and the human being, we see that unity cannot
exist without diversity. Unity and diversity
interpenetrate each other freely. Unity is
diversity, and diversity is unity.

THE WISDOM OF NONDISCRIMINATION

We normally have a dualistic way of looking at the world. We categorize things as good or bad, right or wrong. The wisdom of nondiscrimination is an understanding of the deeper nondualistic nature of things. This way of seeing goes beyond concepts. Classical science is based on the belief that there is an objective reality that exists independently of the mind. In Buddhism, however, there is mind and there are objects of mind, and they manifest at the same time; we can't separate them. In quantum physics, scientists have begun to see that their mind affects the particle they are observing. Objects of mind are created by the mind itself. The way we perceive the world around us depends entirely on our way of looking at it.

LOOKING WITHOUT SEEING

A tree reveals itself to an artist only when the artist can establish a relationship with the tree. If we are not fully ourselves, fully human, we may look at our fellow humans without truly seeing them, just as we may look at a tree and not truly see it. When we are in touch with ourselves, we know how to live in such a way that a beautiful future for the world is possible. The question "Is a human future possible?" is meaningless if we can't see the millions of fellow human beings who are living, suffering, loving and dying around us. Only when we come home to ourselves and get in touch with ourselves can we really see ourselves and others and be in touch with the world around us.

CONTRIBUTING TO THE COLLECTIVE INSIGHT

Mindfulness brings concentration, which in turn brings us insight about how to speak and act. Mindfulness and concentration help us to look deeply into the nature of reality and arrive at the insights of nondiscrimination and inter-being. The best thing we can offer the world is our insight. To live our life in mindfulness and with concentration is to continue to produce insight—for our own liberation, healing, and nourishment, and for the liberation, healing, and nourishment of the world.

UNITY OF MIND AND WORLD

Too often we distinguish between the inner world of our mind and the world outside. But these worlds are not separate. They belong to the same reality. The ideas of inside and outside are helpful in everyday life, but they can become an obstacle that prevents us from experiencing the ultimate reality, which transcends all notions of opposites—inside and outside, birth and death, being and nonbeing. If we look deeply into our mind, we see the world deeply at the same time. If we understand the world, we understand our mind. Neuroscience calls this the unity of mind and world.

NO ENEMIES

When we have been a victim of injustice, we need to look deeply into the ones who have made us suffer to see that they too are victims—of their own suffering, delusion, anger, and fear. We should also look deeply to see how our own beliefs, words, or actions may have contributed to the perceptions others have of us, and to their anger or fear. This kind of understanding brings about transformation. We see the other no longer as our enemy, but as someone who needs help. When we begin to understand them, we suffer less. Sometimes even just a small action can bring a great result. If we respond to hatred and violence with hatred and violence, then hatred and violence will never end. But with compassion and inclusiveness, we can put an end to this vicious cycle.

DIFFERENT PERCEPTIONS OF THE SAME REALITY

Each of our life experiences becomes a seed in our store consciousness. From these seeds prejudices can develop on which we base our perceptions. People can even kill one another due to their different perceptions of the same reality. When we have a wrong perception and persist in maintaining it, we continue to hurt ourselves and others.

SEEING REALITY AS A WHOLE

We distinguish between blossoms, leaves,
and the tree that is the basis of their existence;
but in reality, they are one. The same is true of
humanity and nature. In Chinese ink paintings,
much space is always given to nature, and
human beings are included as a part of nature.
There are many traditions of humankind that
encourage us to look at reality as a whole
rather than to cut it into separate entities.

EMBRACING EACH OTHER

During the war in Vietnam, everyone was
a victim of unintelligent policies, and in our
suffering, we condemned each other and
looked on each other as enemies. But in
fact, we were all the victims of a government
that wasn't acting with wisdom or clarity.
Southerners and Northerners alike were
victims. If we had been able to see that, we
wouldn't have been so angry and we would
have been able to embrace everyone—
Northerners and Southerners, Vietnamese
and North Americans, would have been able
to embrace each other. Our enemy is not man,
but it is our inability to see the situation as it
really is. It is our ignorance, the darkness of
our mind that cannot see the real situation
clearly and so gives rise to wrong perception.

This brought about a senseless war in which we killed each other and created such unspeakable suffering for everyone.

A PEACEFUL HEART

Acts of terrorism come from wrong
perceptions, which have bred fear, anger,
and hatred. Terrorism cannot be destroyed
with guns or bombs, for it lies in the hearts of
human beings. To uproot terror, we need to
begin by looking in our hearts. By calming our
minds and looking deeply inside ourselves
we develop the insight to identify the roots
of terrorism. With insight and compassionate
communication, terrorism can be uprooted
and transformed into love. Our current way
of dealing with terrorism is taking us down
a dangerous path of increasing distrust and
fear. It is time to stop. Let us pause. It is time
to seek true strength and true security. What
would it take for us to be able to reach out
to those who have terrorized us and say:

"You must have suffered deeply. You must have a lot of hatred and anger toward us to have done such a thing. You have tried to destroy us, and you have caused us so much suffering. What misunderstanding has led you to take such an action?" We cannot escape our interdependence with other people and other nations in the world. Let us look deeply and find a path of liberation. It is possible to look at each other again with the eyes of trust, fellowship, and love.

STREAM OF BEING

If you look with the eyes of compassion, you will see all your ancestors within you, with all their strengths and weaknesses, and you will treat your body and consciousness with respect. But as long as you're caught in the idea that this body is you, this mind is you, you underestimate and undervalue yourself. All your ancestors are in you, including their strengths and weaknesses, and the sum of all their beliefs and experiences. When you are free from the notion of self, when you can see yourself, body and mind, as a continuous stream of being, continuing your ancestors in you, including the most brilliant and compassionate ones, then you'll begin to treat your body and mind with respect and it won't be difficult for you to show respect to others.

REMOVING WRONG VIEWS

People thought of Jesus, Mahatma Gandhi,
and Martin Luther King, Jr. as dangerous
people. This was based on wrong perceptions
which gave rise to fear and anger. When
people are full of misunderstanding and fear,
they can do violent things. Great spiritual
leaders like Jesus, Gandhi, and Dr. King were
not angry when they died. They felt compassion even toward the people who killed them,
because they knew their actions were guided
by wrong perceptions, anger, and fear. Our
world needs compassion and understanding,
and the practice of mindfulness is the key
to bringing about more understanding and
compassion. Looking deeply, we remove our
wrong views, and from there understanding
and compassion arise.

HEALING THE WOUNDS
IN OUR HEART

When conflicts arise, whether between two
people, two groups of people, or nations, we
need to stop and question our perceptions.
With the practice of good communication,
loving speech, and deep listening, we can
help each other remove wrong perceptions
so that people are no longer afraid and angry.
This is what we can do to stop wars, prevent
terrorism, end violence, and make peace.
We can't prevent terrorism with bombs and
guns. This only produces more terrorists and
makes terrorism stronger. Each of us has
seeds of understanding and compassion.
Touching the wholesome seeds, you help
them to grow every day. With understanding
and compassion, you will be able to heal the
wounds in your heart and in the world.

LOVE IS THE NECTAR
THAT HEALS

Love enables us to see things that cannot be
seen without love. The eyes of compassion are
also the eyes of understanding. Compassion
is the sweet water that springs forth from the
source of understanding. To practice looking
deeply is the basic medicine for anger, hatred,
and fear.

CREATING A BETTER ENVIRONMENT

Looking deeply at a human being, we see that an individual is made of many more elements than what we normally see. These include the person's parents, ancestors, education, society, and culture. If we don't see all these elements, we haven't fully seen that person. If someone has the tendency to behave in a negative manner, it doesn't mean that they like behaving that way, but that they may be the victim of transmission. These negative seeds may have been transmitted to them by their parents, their culture, or their society. Realizing this, we don't judge them. Instead we feel inspired to change the environment, education, and culture so that the next generation will not be a victim of the same transmission.

ALL OUR ANCESTORS

We know very well that we have ancestors. But our ancestors are not only human. We have animal ancestors, we have plant ancestors, and we have mineral ancestors. Our human ancestors are still very young. We appeared on Earth very late in the history of life. Our animal ancestors are still there in us. The reptile, the fish, and the ape are still in us. Not only were they part of us in the past, but we continue to have them within us in the present moment. Just look deeply into our cells; we see that we are the whole history of life.

THE STREAM OF LIFE

Looking into your body, you will discover that you are not a separate self, cut off from everything else, but that you are a continuously flowing stream—the stream of life itself. The one contains the all. Your body can tell you everything there is to know about the cosmos, boundless space, and time without end. You will see that the here is also the there, and that the now carries within itself the span of eternity, including the past and the future. Eternity is there to be touched in each moment. Both sun and moon, all the stars and all the black holes, can nestle comfortably inside a tiny grain of sand.

ULTIMATE REALITY

Everything we see in terms of being and nonbeing, birth and death is a mental construct. When we look into a cloud with mindfulness and concentration, we touch the nature of no-birth and no-death of the cloud. We can see the cloud as it is, no longer as a fabrication of our mind. The ultimate reality is free from mental constructs and from all notions such as birth and death, being and nonbeing, coming and going, same and different.

NOTHING IS LOST

Looking with the eyes of signlessness will help you to transcend a person's outer form. If you're capable of seeing him or her with the eyes of signlessness, you won't grieve when that appearance is no longer there. Because even when that appearance is gone, your beloved is still there somewhere. Nothing is lost. If we don't have this form, we have another form. If we don't have the cloud, we have the rain. If we don't have the rain, we have the tea. Your body, your presence, and your consciousness occupy all of time and space. In that sense there is no "before" and "after" we die. Generating enough of the energy of mindfulness and concentration, we are able to have this awareness and transcend the notion of birth and death.

SEEING NATURE'S INTELLIGENCE

When we look deeply at a blade of grass,
we can see that it's not mere matter. It has its
own intelligence. A seed knows how to grow
a plant with leaves, flowers, and fruit. A pine
tree is not just matter; it possesses a sense of
knowing. Each atom in a particle of dust has
intelligence and is a living reality. Like each of
the cells in our body, everything has its innate
wisdom. Mother Earth creates, nourishes,
and sustains life, and has infinite wisdom and
intelligence.

TAKING CARE OF THE ENVIRONMENT

We usually discriminate between humans and non-humans, thinking that we are more important than other species. We humans are made entirely of non-human elements, such as plants, minerals, earth, clouds, and sunshine. When we see that humans have no self, we see that to take care of the environment (the non-human elements) is to take care of humanity. For our practice to be deep and true, we must include the ecosystem. If the environment is destroyed, humans will be destroyed, too. The best way to take good care of human beings so that they can be truly healthy and happy is to take care of the environment. Protecting human life is not possible without also protecting the lives of animals, plants, and minerals—the rocks, the soil, the rivers, and the oceans.

TANGERINE MEDITATION

The next time you have a snack like a
tangerine, please put it in the palm of your
hand and look at it in a way that makes the
tangerine real. You don't need a lot of time,
just a few seconds. Looking at it, you can see
a beautiful tree, a blossom, the sun, the rain,
and the tiny fruit forming. You can see the
continuation of the sunshine and the rain, and
the transformation of the baby fruit into the
fully developed tangerine. You can see the
color changing from green to orange and the
tangerine ripening and sweetening. Looking
at a tangerine in this way, you will see that
everything in the cosmos is in it. Peeling the
tangerine, smelling it, and tasting it, you can
be very happy. You can taste the sweetness
of the sun.

AWARE OF OUR FOOD

Before eating, we can look at the dishes
on the table and breathe in and out to see
if this food and drink is good for us and
whether eating it will harm or help develop
our compassion. Each of us can look to see
if we can recognize our deepest desire—Is
it healthy or not? Is it bringing us suffering or
happiness?—because our deepest aspiration
is the food that nourishes our consciousness
and our life. We have to look deeply to see
how we grow our food, so we can eat in
ways that preserve our collective well-being,
minimize our suffering and the suffering of
other species, and allow the Earth to continue
to be a source of life for all of us.

TRULY SEEING

The practice of looking deeply helps us and the people around us to wake up to the fact that we have a beautiful planet that needs our protection. That is why enlightenment, awakening, is very important. If we live mindfully in everyday life, walk mindfully, are full of love and caring, then we create a miracle and transform the world into a wonderful place. Every one of us has the seed of awakening in us, and that is why we are hopeful. Everything we do should be aimed at bringing about collective awakening.

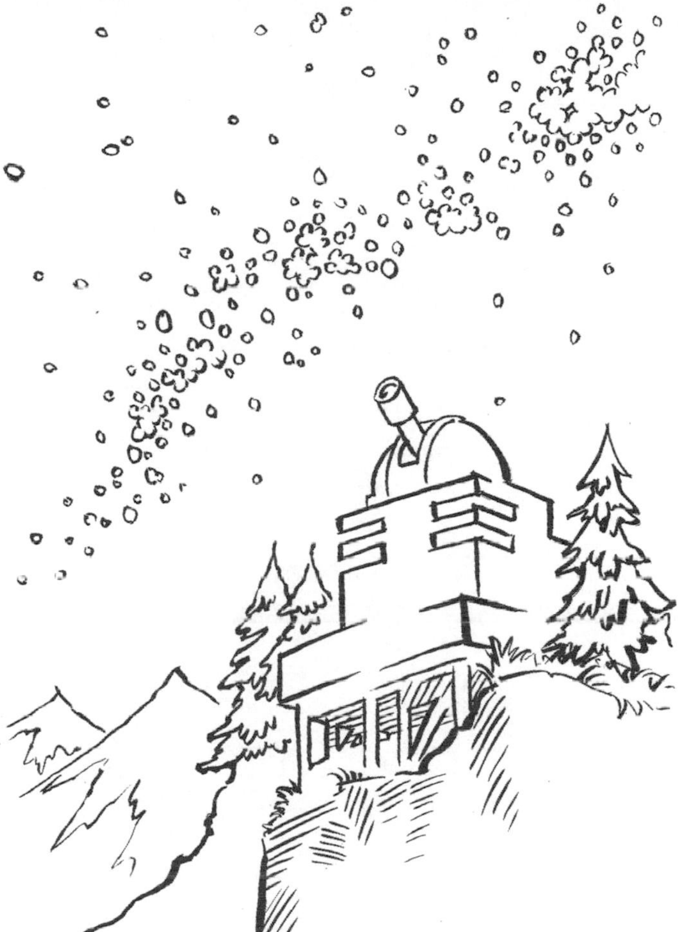

PRACTICES FOR LOOKING DEEPLY

1. THE NOURISHMENT OF MEDITATION

The basic practice of meditation is awareness of breathing. Conscious breathing is the bridge between body and mind. By focusing on our breathing we bring our mind back to our body, and we become truly present, truly alive. Practicing mindfulness of breathing brings calm and peace to body and mind. When body and mind are calm we can see more clearly. We can be in touch with the miracles inside and around us and be nourished by the joy of meditation.

2. SITTING MEDITATION

Find a quiet place to sit comfortably, on a
cushion or a chair, with your back upright but
not rigid. Bring your awareness to your body.
Smiling gently can help relax the muscles in
your face, your shoulders, your whole body.
Bring your awareness to your breathing. Feel
your abdomen gently rising and falling with
each in- and out-breath. If your mind wanders
off, gently invite it back to your breathing
again. Here are some guided meditations you
can practice with. The first line accompanies
your in-breath, and the second line
accompanies your out-breath.

Breathing in, I know I am breathing in.
Breathing out, I know I am breathing out.

Breathing in, I follow my in-breath all the
   way through.
Breathing out, I follow my out-breath all the
   way through.

Breathing in, my breath becomes deeper.
Breathing out, my breath becomes slower.

Breathing in, I relax my whole body.
Breathing out, I smile to every cell in my body.

3. RELEASING TENSION TO BRING CLARITY

We can see and act with clarity when we know how to release the tension and pain in our body. With mindful breathing, body and mind come together, we're established in the here and now, and can more easily handle the situations in our lives. Mindful breathing brings well-being. In one breath we can recognize and release the tension within us.

Breathing in, I am aware of my whole body.
Breathing out, I release all the tension
   in my body.

Breathing in, I am aware of my mind.
Breathing out, I calm my mind.

4. RESTORING CALM

When our mind is disturbed by strong emotions, we're no longer lucid and peaceful, and our perceptions are distorted. When our mind is calm like a peaceful lake, we reflect things as they are.

Breathing in, I know I am breathing in.
Breathing out, I know I am breathing out.

Breathing in, I calm my body.
Breathing out, I calm my mind.

Breathing in, I see myself as still water.
Breathing out, I reflect things as they are.

5. MINDFULNESS IN DAILY LIFE

Mindfulness is an important agent for our transformation and healing. Mindfulness is always mindfulness of something. We can be mindful of our breath, our footsteps, our thoughts, and our actions. Mindfulness requires that we bring all our attention to whatever we're doing, whether walking or breathing, brushing our teeth, or eating a snack. When we concentrate on our breath and the steps we're making, we can see the beauty of the Earth around us more clearly. We can take each breath and each step with awareness and gratitude.

6. WALKING MEDITATION

Mindful breathing and mindful walking can bring a lot of happiness. Walking in a relaxed, peaceful way is healing for body and mind. Let your breathing and your steps nourish you. When you walk, know that you're walking. Don't think about arriving anywhere. Know that you're putting your feet on the Earth. If an irritation arises, simply recognize it and say "Hello, my irritation, I know you are there." Say "hello" and "goodbye," and come back to your steps. Wherever we walk we can practice walking meditation. Many times a day we have to walk from one room to another, from the car to the office, or from the bus stop to the house. Each time is an opportunity to use mindful walking to stop, relax, and be peaceful. Each step can nourish, heal, and bring insight.

7. LOOKING WITH THE EYES OF COMPASSION

Learning to look at others with the eyes of compassion is a wonderful practice. You don't suffer anymore, and your way of looking at others makes them feel better. Each day you can celebrate your twenty-four brand new hours and make the vow to look at all beings with the eyes of compassion.

> Waking up this morning, I smile.
> Twenty-four brand new hours are before me.
> I vow to live fully in each moment
> and to look at all beings with the eyes
>   of compassion.

8. TRUTH IS FOUND IN LIFE

In our community we live by a number of guidelines that help us live happily and in harmony with ourselves, each other, and the planet. They are trainings that help us to be aware of the effects of our actions and words. We read them regularly to help our understanding deepen and insight to arise, so that we know what to do and what not to do to increase happiness and reduce suffering in ourselves and in the world. They are not rules or commandments, but insights born from directly observing suffering and its causes. The first three trainings concern the mind and our way of seeing. They come first because the mind is the root of everything else: our thoughts, perceptions, speech, and actions.

Openness
The First Mindfulness Training

Aware of the suffering created by fanaticism and intolerance, we are determined not to be idolatrous about or bound to any doctrine, theory, or ideology, even Buddhist ones. We are committed to seeing the Buddhist teachings as a guiding means that help us learn to look deeply and develop understanding and compassion. They are not doctrines to fight, kill, or die for. We understand that fanaticism in its many forms is the result of perceiving things in a dualistic or discriminative manner. We will train ourselves to look at everything with openness and the insight of interbeing in order to transform dogmatism and violence in ourselves and the world.

Nonattachment to Views
The Second Mindfulness Training

Aware of the suffering created by attachment to views and wrong perceptions, we are determined to avoid being narrow-minded and bound to present views. We are committed to learning and practicing nonattachment from views and being open to others' experiences and insights in order to benefit from the collective wisdom. Insight is revealed through the practice of compassionate listening, deep looking, and letting go of notions rather than through the accumulation of intellectual knowledge. We are aware that the knowledge we presently possess is not changeless, absolute truth. Truth is found in life, and we will observe life within and around us in every moment, ready to learn throughout our lives.

Freedom of Thought

The Third Mindfulness Training

Aware of the suffering brought about when we impose our view on others, we are determined not to force others, even our children, by any means whatsoever—such as authority, threat, money, propaganda, or indoctrination—to adopt our views. We are committed to respecting the rights of others to be different, to choose what to believe and how to decide. We will, however, learn to help others let go of and transform narrowness through loving speech and compassionate dialogue.

From the Fourteen Mindfulness Trainings of the Order of Interbeing.

OTHER TITLES IN THE SERIES

How to Eat

How to Fight

How to Love

How to Relax

How to Sit

How to Walk

RELATED TITLES BY THICH NHAT HANH

Be Free Where You Are

Being Peace

Happiness

Interbeing

The Long Road Turns to Joy

Making Space

The Mindfulness Survival Kit

No Mud, No Lotus

Reconciliation

The Sun My Heart

Touching Peace

Understanding Our Mind

Monastics and visitors practice the art of mindful living in the tradition of Thich Nhat Hanh at our ten mindfulness practice centers around the world. For a full listing of practice centers, or for information about retreats, visit plumvillage.org or contact:

Plum Village
33580 Dieulivol, France
plumvillage.org

Deer Park Monastery
Escondido, CA 92026, USA
deerparkmonastery.org

Magnolia Grove Monastery
Batesville, MS 38606, USA
magnoliagrovemonastery.org

Blue Cliff Monastery
Pine Bush, NY 12566, USA
bluecliffmonastery.org

European Institute of
Applied Buddhism
D-51545 Waldbröl, Germany
eiab.eu

Thailand Plum Village
Nakhon Ratchasima
30130 Thailand
thaiplumvillage.org

The Mindfulness Bell, a journal of the art of mindful living in the tradition of Thich Nhat Hanh, is published three times a year by our community. To subscribe or to see the worldwide directory of Sanghas, or local mindfulness groups, visit mindfulnessbell.org.

The Thich Nhat Hanh Foundation supports Thich Nhat Hanh's peace work and mindfulness teachings around the world. For more information on how you can help or on how to nourish your mindfulness practice, visit the foundation at tnhf.org.